How to Beat Criticism and Feel Good

Learn to shrug it off and move forward

Awen Finn

Studio 8 Publishing / Sydney

CLAIM YOUR FREE BONUS GIFTS TODAY!

As a big thank you for buying and reading this book,
I'd like to give you some great bonus gifts to help you
on your journey to beating criticism and feeling good.
When you visit the link below, you'll be able to
access resources outlined within this book.
So go ahead now and visit the link below to access all
of your resources

http://readmysongreadmysoul.com/store-2/

Here's just a peek at what you'll receive when you
visit this link:
FREE Templates
FREE Worksheets
FREE Competitions
You can access all this and more today when you
visit:

http://readmysongreadmysoul.com/store-2/

"You can become happy just by deciding to be happy."

    —OSHO

"Don't compromise yourself. You are all you've got. There is no yesterday, no tomorrow, it's all the same day."

    — JANIS JOPLIN

CONTENTS

{ 1 }

Introduction

When were you last criticised? A week ago, a few days ago, or was it yesterday? And why were you criticised? Or to phrase it another way, what was wrong with you? Were you playing music too loudly, taking someone for granted? Were you too fat, too untidy, spend thrifty, distracted, late, or were you simply wearing the wrong outfit? Have you felt the pain and shame of criticism? If you are like me, you have; so I've written this little book to show you that you are not alone and, more importantly, this book offers practical advice and simple techniques to help you beat criticism and feel good. Loving, constructive criticism can be helpful, but let's face it, how much criticism is truly constructive? Oftentimes receiving criticism is unnecessary and hurtful. If you feel like you are drowning from being told what's wrong with you, it may be time to say "Enough!" Isn't it time to reclaim your power and beat criticism? We all deserve to feel good. It's our natural state of being.

{ 2 }

The pain of being human

Pain

You don't deserve... You are... Why aren't you more like your sister? You are a... I am disgusted with you. Get out. You always... I don't like you. YOU. It's your fault. It's not good enough. Look at the state of you. We all think that you... UGH. Go. Nobody wants you.

Pain, it's cruel. It's better to pretend it didn't happen.

What's wrong with me?

Many of us are raised as children with the sinking feeling that there is something wrong with us. We are criticized; we don't measure up. We feel little approval or acceptance. As life progresses, we may hear this criticism from peers, friends, siblings, bosses, and spouses. Critics are everywhere. Parents are trying their best to raise us, but habits play a big part, with many parents unconsciously copying the negative words and behaviours they themselves received as children. Frequently, adults and parents act instinctively and are unaware of the words they are saying or the actions they are doing; it's so easy to absentmindedly voice ten criticisms to someone while giving no words of praise. We are oblivious to the damage we do. It is common to be unaware of ourselves and many of us are guilty of this to some extent or another. How often do we actually think before we talk? It takes enormous courage to stop the roller coaster of criticism, inwardly reflect and wisely choose considerate words. And so there is a huge chance that you, just like me, will also have been on the receiving end of hurtful criticism.

Have I always thought that something is wrong with me? Probably. Actually, that's not true, the answer is yes. But many of us don't often voice this as we secretly feel embarrassed about the answer. And is this is a good thing or a bad thing to think that there is something wrong? Looking back and with hindsight, I don't think it matters. Sometimes we improve our weaknesses, which may help us receive a pay raise at work or become lovelier and help us attract the perfect partner. Sometimes our self-esteem is intact and we skip merrily on our path, unfazed by the barbs launched our way. The lucky ones know there's nothing wrong with them.

However, sometimes we become inert and wish we were somewhere else, preferably somewhere sunny, with a television to keep us entertained and distracted, so we don't feel our pain. We pretend our pain is not there. Other times, we reach for the top shelf bottle, cigarettes, food or pills—it doesn't matter the cure, anything to anesthetize feeling wrong, feeling bad, feeling unloved, feeling unwanted. Anything to feel better, for a while at least.

We all have sensitivities

What are your sensitivities? What are your triggers? What do nasty people say to hurt you? What causes you pain? Physically, are you too fat or too thin? Are your feet too big or is your nose crooked? Mentally, are you a tad slow? What's your general knowledge like? How about your geography? Do you know where Samoa is? Are you color blind? Are you told, once too often, not to give up your day job? Emotionally, are you a cry baby? Sexually, are you too promiscuous or too frigid? How do you stack up? Materially, how big is your pay packet and how many bathrooms does your house have? Academically, what's your score card, As or Cs? Personality wise, are you too lazy, too opinionated, too greedy, too inconsiderate, too unhelpful, too insecure, too proud, or are you off with the fairies? And let's not forget the whole package? Are you good enough? Are you worthy? Are you likeable? Are you lovable?

Does it really matter what your sensitivity is? The list goes on, ad infinitum. It's a lucky dip. Take your pick. Substitute freely. Our sensitivities have only one destination. They all follow the same path, and that's to pain. All of these imperfections and sensitivities come with the same warning: Hazardous. May cause wounds.

My own story

My own sensitivities fall under the big ticket items. As a teenager I was so bad, I was ejected from the family home. Once a month, or even once a week, my father would tell me to leave home. This treatment wasn't exclusive to me and my siblings were individually told to leave too. I arrived at the sad conclusion that there was clearly something wrong with me if my father wanted me out of the house. But, I'm not sure what was wrong with me, so I let it settle into an uncomfortable feeling of badness. I was bad, just like a bad apple. I felt unwanted, discarded, like an old shoe thrown out with the rubbish. Unlovable was a no brainer. Check.

The abyss

I was twelve when I was first thrown out of my family home—a tender age. It was awful. It hurt. This was my introduction to humiliation, shame and pain. I was surprised to be thrown out because I worked hard to be a good girl. I nagged my brothers and sisters a fair bit. I talked back when I shouldn't talk back, especially to elders. I was caught not attending high school in the 6th form, and on one occasion, I ate more than my share of biscuits! I am guilty of these sins, but I'm not sure of the other criticisms I received— and there were a lot of them.

My father had started drinking. He had a full time job in a bank, six kids to support, a working wife and his own childhood demons to contend with. My father also worked hard to be a good boy and sacrificed so that his family could get ahead, all while neglecting his own personal happiness; personal happiness wasn't as necessary or accounted for in the same way it is today. Therapy was unheard of. I'm sure my father felt trapped and burdened. His body couldn't cope with alcohol; the second drink usually sunk my father into a destructive feeling of aggravation and aggression.

Back then people were not taught to question their inner motives and behaviours and few people were taught to cope emotionally, mentally and spiritually with their issues. As with most people, my dad copied the behaviour he had seen and received as a child. He was thrown out of his family home so the automatic response when he felt aggravated was to do this to his own children.

Skipping ahead to my thirties. I became a partner, businesswoman and mother, but apparently, there were still things wrong with me and I was told I needed help. My sensitivities were running amok, along with my intake of alcohol and cigarettes. A psycho-therapist was promptly found for me, presumably to cure my badness, which by this time had morphed into a feeling of craziness. And for me, visiting a psychiatrist confirmed this. My worst fear was becoming real; I was probably mad.

As a consequence of the criticism I received, my emotional intelligence was becoming inhibited. I was desperate to not feel the pain, so I ignored it. I pretended the criticism and pain weren't happening. I didn't know what to do with my emotions. I treated emotions like food; stuffed them down, without chewing, swallowing hard. I pretended it didn't hurt. I fooled everyone. My best friend didn't know.

Feeling bad

Feeling bad is dreadful; it's painful. Pain cuts to the bone and runs deep. I had become adept at locking this pain away, hiding it in a treasure chest deep inside me. My treasure chest of dirty secrets of criticism was so bejewelled and weighted with heavy golden chains, I had no fear that it would accidently spill open and reveal its contents to the world, let alone to me.

However, in life, it is often the case that we are not the ones running the show, even if we think we are and the soul has a mysterious way of taking control when she wants growth, progress and development. Unknown to me, while I was hoarding my quota of badness, wrongness, filth, and pain, my soul had other plans; she was desperate to uncover the mystery of this pain, the reason for this pain. She was desperate to conquer this pain and let it go. I, my physical self, didn't really have a choice. There was no option. Both of us made a pact; it was a blood pact, an energy pact, a mind, body and soul pact. The pain would no longer weigh us down, we would release it, float to the surface, and breath the fresh air of freedom, even if we died trying.

Nasty people

Why are some people nasty? Were they born that way, or have they received their own abuse, criticism and general unfairness to contend with? Have you ever been nasty? I know I have.

Sometimes being nasty to another can relieve the burden of carrying more of our own pain. Pain is weighty stuff. It's like quick sand, it's like drowning, take on too much weight and you will smother. However, I digress; let's keep the focus out there on the villain. After all he's the cause. Shame nasty people are born I guess, shame we are unlucky enough to meet them, I guess. Why can't they be good people like us?

The critic is closer than you think

Critics are everywhere. And your own personal critics are probably very close to you. Critics are frequently husbands, wives, mothers, fathers, brothers, sisters, children, friends and workmates. Bosses and teachers factor in too, but their role is that of supervisor rather than loving family member and social peer. Who are your personal critics? To be fair, there are also minor critics in your life, but they don't hurt you in the same way. You do not hurt deeply nor do you seek their approval in a similar manor to the major critics. We don't fall over, lie down and die if these minor critics don't approve; we can brush it off.

The critic is responding to habit and his own lifetime of receiving criticism

The critic feels pain too. He feels criticised as well. The critic is on the same rotating wheel as us. We are all blindly running, trying to escape the criticism, trying to feel better.

Perhaps it's time to wake up. Perhaps it's time to see and perceive more clearly. Perhaps it's time for compassion. Perhaps it's time to do the work to beat criticism and feel good.

{ 3 }

Tell-tale signs of criticism

Are you conscious or unconscious of what is happening? How does criticism affect you?

Are you awake or are you asleep? Are you conscious or unconscious? We are often unconscious of what is happening to us and within us. We know we feel depressed, sad, unseen and bad, but we don't know why. It's helpful to become aware of what is happening so we can free ourselves from negative habits and reactions. It's helpful to ask ourselves why we are feeling a certain way and to patiently try to uncover the causes and symptoms of our unhappy feelings.

What types of comments make you feel the most upset? Is it a singular word or a phrase which upsets you? Who makes these remarks to you? Are these major sensitivities for you? Can you trace sensitivity of some criticisms to early childhood? Are the criticisms true? Do you believe them? If so, why do you believe them? Are you jumping to conclusions and assuming a criticism even though no criticism was implied? Are you living your life expecting to receive criticism? Notice your responses. When someone gives you a compliment, how do you react? Do you find it difficult to accept compliments?

How about yourself, how do other people react when you criticise them? How often to you generalise negative personality traits and start sentences with, "You always…" How do other people respond when you criticise?

Aim to be a little more conscious. If we were to ask a group of people how aware they are of themselves, many people would say they were quite aware, aware, or very aware. But most of us really aren't aware at all. We have no clue what are habits are. We are tossed around by the whims of life, innocent of how the kinks affect us. We travel through life responding, reacting and mindlessly repeating our old, outworn habits and glib responses. We act on autopilot. Becoming aware of our self and our inner world is hard work. Choosing to reflect inwardly upon our feelings, thoughts, assumptions and beliefs takes a lot of time, effort, attention and practice. It is not easy work.

How do you recognise the tell-tale signs of criticism? Below are some common indicators. Which signposts apply to you?

Approval and acceptance

Approval and acceptance are basic human needs. They are not wants nor are they luxuries. We need to feel that our body, mind, soul and our actions are approved of (most of the time) and we need to feel that we are accepted by our tribe, be it family and peer group or country. When we don't feel approved of or accepted, life can become difficult. In a similar way, it is common to feel rejection at one time or another in our lives. Rejection is painful and criticism can lead to rejection. Does your group approve of you? Does the tribe accept you?

Defenses

You'll know if someone close to you has pressed one of your buttons, one of your sensitivities, because your defenses will rise. You want to defend yourself so that you don't become hurt. You will want to defend yourself so you don't feel disapproval or rejection. Another common response with defense is to launch an attack. When do you defend yourself?

How do you measure up?

Do you compare yourself to others? I sometimes do too. We frequently compare ourselves silently. Comparing ourselves is a no win game. We never measure up. We can never be good enough. What's our criteria for self-comparison? There doesn't seem to be a set list of goodness that we use for comparison. Have you noticed how we change the indicators and basis of comparison? The factors we chose to compare changes as impulsively as our thoughts change.

As a teenager, did you compare yourself in beauty and good looks, or did you compare yourself in intelligence? Did you compare the size of your family home or the income status and prestige of your parent's careers? As a youth did you compare your exam results or your sexual prowess? How about your job? Did you measure up? As a parent, did you compare your kids to each other and to schoolmates? How about their grades? Did they measure up? Do you compare yourself if you are divorced or single or do you compare your wealth and car model and make?

The list goes on. We can't win. Why do we waste our time with this game? We only play the comparison game because it's a habit. The game has a predictable outcome. The game always ends the same way—we feel bad about ourselves. We self-judge; we self-criticise. We feel embarrassed. We don't measure up. We keep quiet about it. We feel too ashamed to admit our perceived faults and weaknesses. And so we have no idea that everyone else is feeling bad about themselves too. We suffer in silence. This self-judgement and self-criticism is a tool of the ego to tell us that we are not good enough. The ego wants to keep us small. The ego doesn't want us to transform into bigger, better, shinier versions of our selves.

When we compare ourselves, when we don't measure up, we criticise ourselves. We are in pain. We need to wipe the slate of comparisons clean if we want to feel good. Now is as good a time as any to start. How do you compare yourself to others?

Our own worst enemy?

Often, we can become so biased and belligerent in our thinking that the only things we notice are disapproval and rejection, even when there is much evidence to show that this is not entirely the case. Many of us are guilty of this at times, seeing the glass half empty. How many criticisms do you receive? How many praises do you receive? Try to be fair with your evaluation. You may surprise yourself. The glass may be half full and you may receive far more praises than criticisms. With criticism do you see the glass half empty?

Sometimes we don't help ourselves. After all, we're good girls aren't we? Unfortunately, many times we find it hard to act with responsibility and empowerment. It can be difficult for us to understand that if we don't have our buttons then we also won't have our corresponding sensitivities. We take the stance that our buttons are permanent and other people shouldn't push them. Often, we are not prepared to look at our buttons and take responsibility for them. We tend to think, it's not our fault. It's those nasty people, criticising us and pushing our buttons. They should know better shouldn't they? What are your sensitive buttons? Are you fed up with them being pushed? Is it time to release them?

What masks do you wear?

A mask helps us to hide from our self and from others. Masks hide our authentic natures.

The subject of masks was introduced to me at Spiritual school. I was attending a training class with about twenty fellow students and we were asked to write down a key adjective to describe each of the students present. Sheets of paper circulated around the group and we recorded the best single adjective to fully describe each of our fellow classmates. At the end of the exercise, our own sheet was delivered to us, and carefully and thoughtfully, written upon this page were the twenty adjectives our classmates saw in us, the qualities we embodied. This exercise was to demonstrate the beauty and virtues held within each of us.

In class, each exercise was usually followed with a discussion and when it was my turn to talk about the adjectives I had received, I burst into tears. Written on my sheet, and repeated many times, was the word 'fun.' I was at spiritual school and I didn't think that the quality 'fun' stacked up well against the more obvious qualities of sincere, pious, devoted and loving. But the question was, why my sudden outburst of tears. Why were my emotions taking over? So the class discussion transitioned into one of masks.

My teacher pointed out to me that 'fun' may be a mask I wear. And when I thought about it carefully, I could see how I used the mask of fun whenever I felt uncomfortable, such as when I was meeting new people. I'd been wearing this mask for a long time, since my childhood. Fun was my go-to demeanour when I didn't want to show my feelings and I used the mask of fun to help me feel confident in a group. When I clearly understood how I was wearing a mask, I no longer needed to use it. This was a revelation for me. I became more authentic. I understood that the group would like me whether I was fun or serious.

The character held in a mask can be personality trait too. The key is to know when you are wearing the quality as a mask and trying to hide yourself. For example, when I was raising my children, I injected a lot of fun into my mothering role, as I enjoy playing and to hear children laugh is infectious. Injecting fun into mothering helped me to feel good and helped my kids feel good too. However, I also had a tendency to wear the mask of fun when I didn't want to reveal my painful feelings.

This story also shows us that there are many opportunities for learning if we remain open. Whenever our emotions are taking over and running the show, it may be helpful, to pause and reflect as to what is really happening inside of us. Who knew an exercise designed to teach beauty and virtues would take a side turn to teach about masks. Do you wear a mask? What are your masks? What persona do you wear to prevent you from being criticised and feeling hurt?

YOU, YOU, YOU and generalities

'Baby, I love you." That's the only time I want to hear the 'you' word. In my opinion, the 'you' word doesn't belong anywhere else other than song lyrics. You'll know what I mean if you've received too many negative 'you' words. Baby join the club, we'll accept you. You are nasty, rude, too short, and smelly ....all of the time. And not only one part of you is this smut....all of you is this smut all of the time (in another words, you're doomed to die and end up in hell.) Why the generalities? Let's be more precise. Let's be kinder and more considerate. Criticise the behaviour and not the person. Say how the negative behaviour makes you feel and then reassure the person that you value them. In this way the sting is gone.

We don't feel so bad receiving the criticism and interestingly enough, neither do the people who issue the criticism. Are you fed up being tagged with too many general 'you are always…' labels?

Addictions

Why is it that some people fall under the spell of addictions, while others dance merrily past without stopping? I have a strong addict tendency and I veer to excess, rather than moderation. Moderation does not seem glamourous to me. I am drawn to big, mythic proportions and dramas.

Addictions can suggest emotional issues and I have had my share of emotional issues. I carried a lot of pain. I started smoking at the age of eighteen and it wasn't long afterwards I was drinking. I don't consume drugs and in this I feel lucky. I vividly remember, at around the age of twenty-two, an inner realisation dawned within me to refrain from drugs as I am sure I would have become a drug addict and would not be alive now if I had succumbed to the temptations. I didn't know at the time that I was hearing my intuition, but I did pay attention and headed the warning. I am thankful for it as I would have easily been susceptible to the charm of drugs.

Why are so many of us addicted to sex, exercise, work and drugs? What lies behind the addiction? Why is it that we can stop one addiction but promptly substitute it with another? Ten years ago, we used to be a society of smokers, but we've stopped smoking and now our girths are expanding.

I tend to agree with the thought process that emotions are a major cause of addictions. I know myself, I would have done anything to zone out and free myself from the ache of pain. For the last ten years or so, I've worked hard in this area; there was no quick fix for me. I started and stopped a few times with cigarettes, finally quitting on my fourth try and even today I'm diligent, ever watchful, working hard with my will, ever vigilant to the seductions of addiction.

Addictions are a tell-tale sign of pain. Please get help if you want to feel better.

Another big one—Guilt

Do you suffer from guilt? Do other people make you feel guilty? Have you committed a wrongdoing?

Guilt can be a good thing. Feeling guilt can help us live up to and practise standards that are important and valuable to us. Guilt can help us grow into better versions of ourselves. As with most things, guilt has both a good side and a bad side.

Guilt lies silently within us and usually warning bells do not sound when we feel this guilt. Many of us have been raised to be good children and we have worked hard to live up to the expectations of our parents and role models. However, we are trying to achieve benchmarks which have been given to us and are not of our own choosing. If you look carefully, you may notice that you often use the word, 'should' when you are trying to live up to these benchmarks. It may be an option that whenever you hear yourself use the word should, as in, "I should do..., or I should be..." that you slow down and consider if it is really important and if it is not important or valuable to you, then perhaps choose not to do this task or attempt to embody this attribute. Your time is valuable. Your happiness is valuable. If you are weighed down with too many external standards and benchmarks that keep you in a state of feeling guilty, then perhaps now may be the time to let some of these standards go. The benefit to you is that you will feel better.

Another area where you may succumb to guilty feelings is when a nasty person indicates, either overtly or subtly, that you are responsible for their own negative behaviour. Sometimes this may be the case, but frequently your own behaviour and actions are not responsible for the negative actions and behaviours of the nasty person. Choose not to feel guilty if the situation has nothing to do with you. Do not listen if the nasty person blames you for their own inability to manage themselves. I have a tendency to feel guilty and so I now try to pay attention whenever this is happening. I slow down and reflect. If my behaviour and actions are not at fault, I release the guilty feelings immediately and if necessary, I calmly voice my innocence. It is not necessary to feel criticised when we are not guilty.

Rumination, round and round we go…

Do you ruminate? Does your mind ceaselessly repeat the slide show of the bad times? My own favourite time to ruminate was along with a packet of cigarettes, which was half empty by the time I'd finished my rumination fix.

Look closely at the rumination. Does it solve anything? No. Do you gain new insight? No. You've seen the slide show before, you know how it ends. Rumination clutters, fogs and obscures your mind, thoughts and energy with the bad times. There's no room left for the good to get in. The fact is, rumination is a waste of your time. It's time you waste feeling bad, while you have the option to spend your time feeling good. There is a quick fix for rumination; stop doing it and park your mind somewhere else. All you need to do is practise placing your mind somewhere else, somewhere happy. Think of all the time you'll save giving up the rumination game, and if you're like me, the money you'll save on those cigarettes.

Self-sabotage

The saboteur is a crafty character. The saboteur is an internal voice that doesn't want us to act or behave in the best way for us, rather, the saboteur wants us to do things that are not in our best interest. Why do we sabotage ourselves? Why do we keep giving up what we know to be good for us? Why are we so averse to putting in the effort? If we stay the same and don't change, our pain stays with us and doesn't change. The saboteur is out to make our life miserable. He wants us to fail. He enjoys quick fixes and laziness. He likes us being small. He is comfortable with us being less than we are meant to be. He enjoys running the show.

Great people progress. They become the best version of themselves. They don't talk. They act. They align their will with where they want to go in life, who they want to be and what they want to achieve. Watch for your saboteur like a hawk. He's out to get you. If the saboteur wins the first round, and stops you doing something which is good for you then stand up in the ring and fight again. Sometimes our saboteur will knock us down a hundred times, and it doesn't get any easier with each knock. Choose standing back up and fighting your saboteur as your new habit and you will eventually feel good. In your life where does your saboteur rule the roost? In which areas do you find it difficult to exert effort to change? Are you prepared to harness your willpower and change old habits that no longer serve you?

The victim

Are you a victim? Are the nasty people the perpetrators? Many of us prefer to play the victim role because the victim role has more prestige than the aggressor role. The victim receives the attention and the sympathy. Who wants to be the bully? Do you even know anybody who has admitted to being a bully?

I was marvellous at playing the victim role. Once again my flair for drama came in handy. Poor me. I spent a whole decade playing the 'poor me' role. It was only when I fully realized that the victim role had no more power than the aggressor role, that I ceased playing the victim part.

If you would like to stop playing the victim, it can be helpful to learn how to use boundaries, both physical boundaries and the intention of boundaries to protect yourself. Consider how you phrase the intention of your boundaries. How often do you let something happen that you don't want to happen? Often, we put up no resistance. It may surprise you to find your power. You are responsible for yourself. Try to put yourself in a safe space and a safe situation. For example, if you are due to meet with family and you feel anxious and at risk to words which may be said, be safe. Don't go. You have the power to say no and to place yourself in a safe situation. Nowadays, I don't know many smokers, but I act safely around the ones that do smoke. I act with responsibility to old addictions and ensure I can exit the friendly gathering easily if I sense any signs of temptation.

It's also a good idea to write down all the benefits you receive playing the victim role, such as attention, kindness, sympathy, and consideration from others.

The list goes on. The victim can be a seductive role. Often victims are excused from trying hard to progress in life.

Some people have good reason to be a victim. Their pain runs deep. However, if you are playing a role to benefit yourself, perhaps realize that you can acquire those benefits elsewhere.

Also, carefully consider where you play the aggressor role. Who do you victimise?

If you receive too much criticism you could well be playing the victim role. If you are a victim you are in pain and don't feel good.

Jealousy from others....spot it but don't focus on it

Sometimes you may find that someone is jealous towards you and criticises you. This person is trying to pull you down while artificially inflating themselves. Try not to become caught up in the drama. Try to be detached. Try to excuse yourself. You don't need to listen to jealousy from others.

Karma

Does karma play a part in the pain? Are our past actions the reason that we receive so much criticism and pain in this life? It depends on your beliefs. I believe that beliefs are choices, not always truths. Choose to believe that which helps you.

Exceptions-constructive criticism

Many of us are under the false illusion and think that when we ourselves are criticising, we are giving constructive criticism. However, we are often negligent and clumsy in the delivery of the constructive criticism and the other person feels hurt. Some of us fool ourselves with the refrain, 'I'm just being honest,' when we criticise. If you are hurting someone when you criticise, please be mindful. No one likes to feel pain or deserves to feel pain because of your belief that you are being honest. Better yet, perhaps choose to practice silence. Silence is a gift of the gods. Take the high road and leave criticism to others.

Constructive criticism from a trusted source is hugely helpful and this can be a speedy path to overcome our weaknesses. If you want to be a good friend, remember to veil your constructive criticism with kindness, consideration and care. This will be a huge help.

If you are sensitive and receive a lot of negative criticism it can sometimes be difficult to spot the constructive advice. Try to slow down your thinking and try to not feel bad about yourself. Check that you feel safe in both the environment and with the person offering the constructive criticism. Go slowly. This can be a tricky situation. Perhaps you are not ready for constructive criticism right now. Be patient. Be kind to yourself.

Special care

Some people are unlucky and unacceptable things happen to them; for other people, life events may be traumatic. If this is the case, this book is not for you. Perhaps you need specialized help. Please go and seek the best help you can find, be it physical, mental, emotional, or spiritual help. You deserve to feel good and I wish you peace.

{ 4 }

What part do you play in the criticism drama?

Inner critic

Often we are our own worst enemies. Perhaps, you believe some nonsense about yourself. I know I do. We have negative opinions about ourselves and that's why we criticise ourselves. What negative opinions do you harbour about yourself?

Many of us are also seduced with the concept of perfection. We use perfection as an excuse to criticise ourselves further. A good example of this is weight. No matter what our weight, we may tend to think that we are a bit big. Whether we are ten kilos lighter or heavier we may think this. Our weight will never be perfect because we keep shifting the goalposts of our desired weight. As we lose weight, our goal weight drops too. We can't catch our goal weight as it is dropping at a faster rate than we shed the pounds. Perfection is a no win game. There is no point waiting for the perfect condition, outcome or result. Be realistic. Perfection probably isn't going to happen.

Refrain from talking pessimistically to yourself. If you are ten kilos lighter, that's great. Be happy. Stop beating yourself up, hoping to achieve a perfect number on the scale. You'll be glad you did and you'll feel much better.

Old, outworn standards

Why do we hurt ourselves? Why do we reinforce standards, which perhaps we didn't choose ourselves and which are well past there expiration date?

A popular standard to which we never measure up is being good. Most of us were raised to be good boys and girls, but unfortunately, not many of us made the grade. Trying to be a good girl or good boy is slavery. Give up the ghost. You will never be good enough. None of us was given a profile description of what being good entails and the people we are trying to impress with our good behaviour haven't got a clue of what being good means either. It's a no win game. None of us has an idea of the goal posts of goodness. How can we pass the goodness test if we don't know the parameters? If you are trying to be good, you probably won't be good enough and someone will criticise you.

And how about 'Yes.' Are you a 'yes' girl? Do you keep saying 'yes' because you don't want to let others down and because you think it is good to help others? Or do you have a need to be needed? Give it up. We always let people down at some stage or other. That's life. I learnt a great lesson with my psychoanalyst, Emma. She reminded me that when we are in an aeroplane and the air pressure drops, the pilot asks us to put our oxygen masks on first. Only then, when our own oxygen mask is fitted properly and we are breathing easily, are we able to help otters. The simple take away is to help yourself first, before you help others. It took me a long time to learn this lesson and this lesson has been of enormous benefit to me. I no longer feel guilty when I say no.

Perhaps your standards need an overhaul. Pick a new current set of values which work for you and reflect where you are in life and who you want to be. Measure yourself against these values and throw the old, outworn, habitual values away. You will no longer need to achieve standards that don't matter. You'll feel lighter when you refrain from criticising yourself needlessly. You'll feel good. You will be a better role model too.

Observe yourself—who and how do you criticise?

Here's an experiment: For a day, carry a notepad and pencil with you. Write down a list of all the people and things you criticise and why. Do you criticise the lady walking out, absent minded, in front of your car? Do you criticise the sales attendant for serving the customers in the queue so slowly, as naturally, you'll be late for work? And do you criticise the alarm clock for not ringing that particular morning causing you to sleep in? You get the idea. How do you criticize objects and situations? What and who do you blame? Watch closely for the criticism you give to people close to you and to family members. You may be surprised to find that perhaps you're not quite the little angel you thought you were.

Also, on the flip side, are you criticising these people and events or instead, are you only feeling frustrated, irritated, exasperated or angry. Or are you doing both? Sometimes we can be feeling frustrated, but we are not criticising at the same time. Conversely, sometimes others may be expressing their irritation but not actually criticising us. Sometimes we can jump to the conclusion of a criticism without it being present or existing.

We criticise those we are close too

Pay special attention to the criticism you give to your family and close friends. Is there a theme running in your criticisms? How do your close buddies respond? Do they jump to your defense? Do they counter with an attack? Do they feel hurt? Do they mask the hurt? Do they feel resentment? Whatever is happening may be an exact replica of how you respond to criticism too.

The mirror—watch yourself

The concept of 'the mirror' is a fascinating tool which can help us. I was given this following exercise with 'the mirror 'at spiritual school and I found it really helpful.

Take an A4 sheet of paper and draw a line down the middle to divide it. Think of a person you like and admire and write out a list of all the qualities you like about this person. Next, think of a person you dislike and list all of the undesirable qualities you notice in this person. Finally, go to the title of each list and cross out the name of the person you imagined and thought about during this exercise and replace their name with the word 'me.'

You may feel uncomfortable reading the list of the qualities you dislike, especially as these undesirable qualities now belong to you. With careful consideration and refection try to discover these aspects within yourself. It can similarly be surprising with the list of qualities we admire and we may have to dig deep to acknowledge that these admirable qualities are also within us. Who knew we were so nice!

The mirror exercise is demonstrating the concept of, 'What you see is what you are.' You are probably all of those good things you have written on your list along with all of the bad things. Look hard and see if you can find these qualities in you.

Why is it that we label some characteristics as good while we label other traits bad? Many traits are both good and bad. It just depends on perspective and who is assessing the particular trait. For example, some people may assess the characteristic of 'aggression' as unlikable. An individual may group the quality 'aggression' with 'domineering' and 'abusive.' Conversely another person may evaluate the characteristic of aggression as a helpful asset as aggression may help to achieve that which we desire. There are many different perspectives and numerous differing ways of evaluating and assessing personality traits. However, we foolishly believe that the way we assess is the only way or the right way. Have you noticed that when we criticise, we witlessly believe that our own traits are good while the other person has the bad traits?

Why is it that we admire some people while at the same time, we are unable to admire ourselves? Why do we spot undesirable qualities so easily in others? Perhaps we have learnt to disown our own negative characteristics and instead project these bad characteristics onto others. Perhaps we have learnt to disown our own positive characteristics and qualities too.

Pay attention to the good in others and you will feel good

Returning to our list in the previous exercise, look through your list of all the things you like and appreciate in your nice person. How do you feel recognising these wonderful qualities? Do you feel good that you can spot these qualities in others? If it's true that 'You reap what you sow,' then why not pay attention to the qualities you like, admire and appreciate in others and why not tell them. Keep practising this praise and wait patiently for the tide to turn. Others will eventually notice your good will to them. They will notice your praise, gratitude and appreciation. They'll want to give it a go too. You will become their role model. It feels good telling people what you like about them and takes the focus away from criticism.

Putting our best foot forward

Put your best foot forward. Concentrate on you. You have the power and choice to change yourself, but it's a fool's game to think you will change others. Go slow. Be kind to yourself. Expect mistakes and slip ups. The secret is continual practise. Theory doesn't really help. Knowing how to do something, being able to do something and doing something are different things. Don't waste your time with theory. You won't win.

Fear

Many of us are fearful of the unknown. What happens to us when we die? We don't know. Change is also frightening for many of us. It's possible that people closest to you may not want you to change. However, it's your life. If like me, you can't bear the chains that bind you then change is on the horizon. Walk tall and greet it with a warm embrace. You have nothing to lose and everything to gain. And you'll feel better.

i

{ 5 }

180-Degree Turn

Happiness

Are you happy? Do you want to be happy? What does happiness look like to you? What's stopping you from being happy?

What do you need to be happy and what do you want to achieve? Is criticism stopping you?

Receiving criticism is painful. It's an energy drain and takes up a lot of our time. This is the same precious time available to spend creating the life we desire. We think about the criticism we have received.

We ruminate. Silently or verbally we defend ourselves. We don't want to be criticised. Underneath the criticism we experience the dreadful feeling that we are not good enough, or not lovable. This ache is persistent. It doesn't leave and so we spend even more time either pretending the ache isn't there or thinking continuously about this painful ache and why we feel so bad. There's no time to be happy; our time is taken up with the criticism. We have no clarity to focus on what we want; we are too busy focusing on the criticism which we don't want. Is it any wonder so many of us are not happy?

Change—it's a fool's game

The best way to stop this merry-go-round of criticism and feeling bad is to be intentional and proactive. It's time for change, but it is precisely at this point where we are most likely to slip up. Why? Because we are still clinging to the outdated belief that we can change other people. We think that if we make a few adjustments in our requests and mode of delivery, we will be able to change the nasty person who criticises us. However, we have forgotten to realize that throughout our life we have never been able to change the nasty person. We have absolutely no experience successfully changing nasty people and we have absolutely no hope to change nasty people in the future. Thinking that we can change others is a fool's game and it's a game we will never win.

A new strategy

It's clear that we need a new strategy. We need to change.

In life, we have concerns. Our power lies in the area of influence we have over these concerns. For example, we may have a camping trip planned for the weekend. We may feel concerned about the weather during the trip, hoping that it will remain dry and sunny. However, we do not have any influence over the weather. The only person who has influence over the weather is Mother Nature, not us. So it is clear that worrying about the weather or having concerns over the weather for the upcoming camping trip is a needless waste of our time as we are unable to influence the weather conditions.

In the same way, we worry and feel concern when we are criticised and feel bad. We are concerned because the criticism is showing no signs of abating. The only area we have influence over this concern about criticism is ourselves.

Let's stop the merry-go-round

If you are unhappy, if you are dissatisfied with the criticism you receive, then it's time to stop the rumination and the negative thinking about the criticism and to replace this valuable time with thinking happy thoughts about what you want and need to be happy in life. It's a simple switch, but it is tricky to do. We have many years of habit concentrating on the criticism we receive.

The payoff

What's the benefit to you if you choose to change? What's the benefit to you if you choose to change your thinking? What's the benefit to you if you choose to take responsibility for the criticisms you receive? What's the benefit to you if you choose to stop feeling bad? After all, we lose all of the benefits of victimhood if we choose to stop focusing on the criticism and the nasty person who criticises us.

Perhaps at the moment, the new benefits are similar to taking a lucky dip. Perhaps, at the moment it is difficult to discern the new benefits. Do you know what happiness looks like for you? Do you know how you will be and act when you are happy? Are you familiar with the experiences you need to be happy? Do you know the type of relationships which will make you happy and the material possessions which will make you happy?

Is the happiness you seek your own picture of happiness or have you adopted someone else's vision of happiness? Are you playing the support character in the happiness drama of others? Sometimes we are so busy playing the support role in the dramas of others that we have forgotten to include the starring role in our own happy ever after story.

What do you want? Where are you going to put your focus with your reclaimed time?

We all desire to feel happy, fulfilled and successful. We want to feel our lives mean something.

Dreams and aspirations as a child remind us of our purpose

Here's an exercise to help remind you of what you may need or want to be happy.

Try to remember your early years. What were you like as a child? What were your natural predispositions and inclinations as a child; did you like reading, making things, cooking or study? How did you interact with people as a child? Did you prefer one on one communication, or were you sociable? Did you take the lead?

Jot down the images and impressions you receive. This will help to reawaken your natural happy inclinations. Perhaps you liked sport and exercise, or tending a garden. Perhaps you liked playing Doctors and nurses or you remember dreams of a four bedroom house with a white picket fence. You may have enjoyed solitude and time alone or you may have preferred being the centre of attention. As a child I always had a best friend and this preference has remained with me throughout adulthood. I have a strong inclination to a one on one relationship rather than a group. Also, as a teenager I was magnetically drawn to the arts and creative expression. And so, is it any wonder that I worked in the art field for 20 years?

Try to write down as much detail as you can. It's possible that you have been thrown off course and the criticism has derailed you. Perhaps you feel depressed about your life and don't know how to start being happy. This exercise is a good place to start. Be patient and kind to yourself. Repeat this exercise as often as you need to. It will help to reawaken your purpose in life.

What are the dreams you imagined as a child?

Delegating happiness

I sometimes delegated choosing my own happiness and I often found it difficult to decide between one creative experience and another. It was well established within me to be a good girl, to sacrifice and to consider the satisfaction, approval and happiness of others ahead of my own. The consequence of this developed as an amenable style of personality, I'd go with the flow. I was 'easy going.' I was fascinated meeting my partner Mick. He was adventurous and exciting. He had big audacious goals—freedom, independence, business, wealth, travel, living outside the box—and he felt a strong desire to live his own life. I was easily seduced and claimed these aspects, achievements and avenues of happiness for my own. I was a hard worker and adept at swallowing any uncomfortable emotions I felt along the way. I didn't give my happiness any other thought. Looking back, it's clear that I would need a crisis to discover my own formula for happiness. And I was lucky. A crisis happened.

Favourite songs—what is your soundtrack to happiness?

During my own crisis of self-discovery I would often look for confirmation that I was selecting the most necessary and also desirable qualities of happiness for me. It is not always easy and obvious what happiness means to us and so I would seek confirmation to ensure I was on the right path. Sometimes I was surprised to find that some pursuits looked exciting and desirable but with reflection I came to realize that these pursuits wouldn't always make me happy. I can now see that I was really trying to discover the absolutely necessary, non-negotiable areas of happiness I needed to experience rather than the glamorous choices and desires of happiness.

I loved astrology and numerology, so I'd often look to these sources to check I was on course and also to further help me ponder alternative nuggets of happiness which I hadn't considered. I remember that my astrology mentioned spirituality, but I had no concept of what this meant, as I was brought up as a good Catholic girl, and so, I assumed spirituality meant religion. And I was not into religion.

There are different approaches to find solutions to our problems and the same approach doesn't work for everybody. The trick is to find the approach which works for you. I was finally able to perceive the concept of spirituality in a different way, rather than solely as religion, using and working with my own self-discovery tool of Song Reads and I chose to trust that spirituality was a necessity for my own happiness. My own Song Read clearly pointed out to consider moving into the spiritual life and at the time, spirituality was not something I had on my happiness list. Perhaps I'm writing this as a shameless promotion for Song Reads or a shameless promotion for astrology. Nevertheless my aim is to highlight that we don't all know what will make us happy, even if we feel embarrassed admitting this. Spirituality was not on my happiness list, I needed Song Reads to highlight this for me. So please don't feel foolish if your happiness list isn't too glamorous or is incomplete; you simply have further self-discovery to do.

Our happiness lists also change with the times. A good happiness list is firm, but fluid. Like many of us, I added happy children, happy parenting and happy mothering to my list. But I didn't know in my youth that I'd have children. I wasn't planning on them, so children were absent from my happiness list in my twenties.

Are you running away from your own gifts and talents?

Choosing to follow our calling is hard work and effort. Choosing our own happiness is hard work and effort. This may sound trivial, but many of us abdicate the good times. We delegate our own happiness without taking responsibility for it. No wonder we are derailed with criticism. Isn't it time you started focusing and thinking of what you want and need to be happy instead?

It's time to reclaim your power

What is your happy list? Find a clean piece of writing paper and hold onto this for dear life. This blank sheet of paper is going to become filled with your future.

What is your happy list? Start to write it down. Use words, sentences, drawings, and doodles. Don't worry about spelling errors or smudges as this list is for your eyes only. Write down anything you are consciously aware of which you know will make you happy. Is running your own business going to make you happy? Or how about living in another country, Africa perhaps. How about money? Do you need five-star hotels to be happy or would you be just as happy camping. How about career, what career will make you happy, which skillsets and talents do you enjoy using? How about relationships. Do we need a fabulous relationship to be happy? Or do you need lots of independence and freedom to be happy? How about children. Do children make you happy or do they make you snappy. Surely you want health to make you happy. Do you enjoy the company of friends or are you happier being by yourself? Are there any special virtues or characteristics which make you feel happy, such as laughter and spontaneity? Don't forget to add the word 'love.'

Now add to your happy list any intuitions you've received, guidance you've received, tips and suggestions from astrology, numerology, Song Reads, or any of these mystery traditions you enjoy and trust.

Also add comments and suggestions from trusted family members, friends and favourite teachers. Have any of them said anything favourable about you which has stuck with you. I still remember my high school art teacher, Mrs. Furley, saying to my parents at open night, that I was the most creative student she had ever taught. She didn't say 'the best,' the 'most proficient' or the 'most commercial.' She used the word creative. This word had stayed with me and it sits happily on my happy list.

Think back to your childhood. Are there any secret gems of happiness here for you? Add them to your list.

Happy List Quadrants

Try to write some happy goals in each of these four Happy Goal Quadrants: health, relationships, career and finance and the quadrant of personal fulfilment.

Then attempt to cross reference these happy goals amongst the four life STYLE Quadrants of physical happiness, mental happiness, emotional happiness, and spiritual happiness.

For example, you may desire warm, happy, nurturing relationships with your children. This happy goal may appear in either of your Happy Goal Quadrants, relationships or personal fulfilment. Pick the quadrant which works best for you. Then cross reference and copy this happy goal into a corresponding life STYLE Quadrants, either physical happiness, mental happiness, emotional happiness or spiritual happiness. In this case let's select the emotional happiness quadrant. Once again, try to choose the quadrant which speaks best to you. We are not aiming at perfection with these happy list quadrants, rather, we are aiming to have further insight into ourselves.

Keep this happy list with you and whenever you gleam new insights into what really make you happy, add this to your quadrants. Strange as it may seem we sometimes are not aware of physical possessions, emotions or experiences which make us happy. How can we know the thrill of skydiving will make us feel happy unless we have done it? I recently added the word, 'peace' to my happy list. I'd never really been consciously aware that 'internal peace' made me feel happy. I was far too busy thinking about active pursuits. I liked the feeling I had after meditation, but I couldn't put a word to the sense I was feeling. It finally dawned on me, out of the blue, that I need and desire to feel peace for my happiness.

You'll also find as you learn more and more about yourself, that you may change the quadrants you place happy goals in. For example, I used to write my desire 'freedom;' in the career and finance quadrant and cross reference this to the physical happiness life STYLE quadrant. However, as I progress on my spiritual journey I now write 'freedom' in the personal fulfilment happy goal quadrant and cross reference this to the spiritual life STYLE quadrant. Different pursuits and belongings have different meanings for us. There is no right or wrong, but for me, moving freedom to the spiritual happiness life STYLE quadrant has helped me to release my own internal criticisms about financial freedom or career freedom. The freedom I really seek is spiritual freedom; it just took me a long time to become aware of this.

Be patient and you may be surprised at some of the items you add or move around your happy list. For an example of how to complete your Happiness List, head over to my blog http://readmysongreadmysoul.com, where I share some of the happy goals on my own list. This is not an exhaustive list; it's an example of how to begin. Don't worry if some of your quadrants are bursting at the seams with happy desires, while other happiness quadrants lie empty. If I had completed this happy list ten years ago, my emotional happiness quadrant would have contained very little, due to my lack of self-awareness, and my spiritual quadrant would have been an empty void.

Rally your courage, you can do it, you are worth it

Develop resilience, develop fortitude. After all, it's your life. Why be a victim and succumb to criticism? Find out what will make you happy and you'll notice that much of the criticism you receive has nothing to do with what makes you happy. This criticism usually belongs to the nasty person that said it, not you. Every time you succumb to old, outworn, negative habits or fail to achieve new goals, every time you become distracted with criticism, stand up and fight. Fight mentally and choose to focus your mind on your own happiness. It doesn't matter how bloodied and bruised you become, when you are troubled by the criticism of others, stand up and fight for your happiness. Focus on your happiness and let the criticism go. Release the criticism. It's your life. Choose to take responsibility for it.

{ 6 }

Solutions Macro View (Birds-Eye view)

The healing journey

We've all heard the term, 'The Hero's Journey,' and some of us even studied it in school. But what about 'The Healing Journey?' I for one can vouch for the Healing Journey. I've experienced this. Looking back I can now see that the crises that happened, the bad things that happened in my life, not only hurt me and caused pain, but they also caused me to reflect, examine, consider and perceive different options and avenues and to ultimately heal. Healing is wonderful. We shake off the cloak of baggage we carry; we shake off the pain. It is hard work. This feeling of lightness does not come free. It does not come easy. Blood, sweat and tears go into the silken gossamer fabric and substance of healing. Why did I choose to heal? I couldn't bear the pain and criticism. I was sinking in the quick sand. I couldn't breathe. I was desperate to get better. Are you?

Standing in your own power

Eventually, you will arrive in this sweet spot. Eventually, you will stand in your own power. Firm and steady like a tree. You will be both rooted to Mother earth and connected to the heavens. You will be secure. You will know your own value. You will sway gently with the breeze, but your branches will not break with the snap of negative criticism.

Objects of beauty...where is the blemish?

In due course you will see that everything is beautiful. Everything is made of the same essence. There is no blemish. Only the blemish of beauty. Perfection is imperfection. Compassion will awaken and you will know and understand that there is no need to

thoughtlessly criticise and there is no reason to receive hurtful criticism either.

Appreciation and gratitude

Most of us have been taught to treat others how
we, ourselves would like to be treated. However, perhaps sometimes like me, you understand the theory
and comprehend this concept intelligently, but forget
to practise this concept. Unfortunately for us, understanding concepts alone does not create change. We
need to do the hard work to reshape our actions and
behaviours to create change. If we want to treat others
well we may need to form a new habit. If we want the
criticism to stop and in its place to receives loving
kind comments and remarks, we perhaps need to
practise offering appreciation to others first.

A good starting place for change is to practise appreciation and gratitude daily. This will help to train
your mind to see, capture and focus on the positive
qualities in other people. A simple exercise to change
this habit is to take a fresh sheet of paper and either
write down 25 things you are grateful for or 25 qualities you appreciate in someone close to you. Here's an
example:

I am grateful my son emptied the dishwasher last night.

I am grateful to have the time to spend one hour walking along the beach this afternoon.

I appreciate and like that my partner is a fabulous home cook.

I appreciate and am grateful that my brother surprised me with concert tickets for Saturday night. I can't wait!

Don't worry if you can't think of twenty-five things. Start with five or ten qualities and build up from there. Commit to practising this exercise daily as it takes time to form new habits. Be persistent. Focus on the good in people.

Forgiveness

This could well be your number one remedy to feeling good. How easily do you forgive? Some people find it difficult to forgive and even voice the refrain, "You've hurt me so much that I could never forgive you." Some people hurt us. Some people are nasty. However, this is our life and we may unwittingly spend far too much time focusing on this hurt. Spending our time thinking and focusing on what the other person has done to us, binds our energy. Our energy has no space to allow the good things in life to enter. Forgiving someone does not mean that we approve of or condone the behaviour of the nasty person, but it does mean that we unbind our own energy. Forgiveness releases our energy and attachment to the perceived wrongdoing. Our energy is free to pursue our happy list. We feel good. We feel peace.

Within a week of my first child being born, I sensed intuitively that it was time to forgive my father for throwing me out of the family home whenever he was in a bad mood. I was a new mother and I was unwilling to carry this old outworn family dynamic into my new family. I wanted a clean slate. I wanted to consciously choose how I would parent my child. I wanted my childhood pain gone. I wanted freedom from the pain. So, I penned a sincere letter of forgiveness to my father. Amazingly my attachment to my childhood distress left me. In its place, I felt compassion for my father. My father kept this letter of forgiveness in his bedside drawer until he passed away. It obviously meant something to him too.

Give forgiveness a go. Forgiveness does not condone the other person's behaviour, but it does release you. Difficult as it is to comprehend, the nasty person is probably doing the best she can. I don't cook very well. I just try the best I can. A lot of the food I cook doesn't taste nice. In the same way, the nasty person is perhaps doing the best she can. He probably can't help that his best isn't to a satisfactory standard.

Calm mind

For me, this is probably the lynch pin of the solution to beating criticism—a calm mind. Calmness creates clarity, consideration, courage and confidence. With a calm mind we are able to listen attentively. We pay attention to tone and body language. We pay attention to the choice of the words said. We pause and reflect. We respond rather than react. We are mindful of our boundaries and able to position ourselves into a safe space, physically and emotionally. We respond assertively rather than aggressively. We maintain peace. We don't need to become hooked into the criticism, we are able to side step it. We practise detachment. These are the benefits of a clear mind. So, it can be helpful to try to cultivate a bright, unclouded, light filled, clear mind.

Meditation to create calmness

Meditation is my go-to saviour. It is one of my priority actions each day and I try to meditate most days. Whenever I feel a lot of anxiety or find myself in stressful situations I try to meditate twice a day. Meditation has abundant benefits, one of which is to help create a clear mind. It takes the same effort to meditate daily whether meditating for thirty-minute or fifty-minute sessions. Many people find the self-discipline needed to form a new habit tricky; after all there are so many distractions; work, television, social media and cooking to name just a few. The choice to meditate boils down to one thing—do you want to feel better? If you are like me and desperate to release the pain and feel better, and think, feel, or sense that meditation may be a solution for you then it may be time to commit to a daily meditation practise.

In my opinion, if you are only going to enact one thing in this book, then let this be the item you action. There's plenty of information on meditation on the market, pick one style and start. I started my meditation journey with a relaxing guided 'yoga nidra' meditation and I still like to practise guided spiritual meditations. Guided meditations enable you to listen to a teacher's voice which gently guides you on where to focus your mind. When meditating, your mind will probably wonder off and become distracted a fair bit. Whenever this happens, just bring your mind back to the meditation and resume your meditation practise.

Meditation is powerful. It helps. For some people the benefits of meditation will be instantaneous, while for others it may take sustained effort to create calmness. Regardless, the benefits of meditation will continue to accrue as you develop your practise over time and over years. If you would like to try a beginner's meditation, please visit my blog to download an audio meditation.

Reactions versus responses to criticisms

Whenever we hear something we don't like, we still have a choice in our reply. We may choose to react or respond. When you are criticised, how often do you react quickly and run to your own defense? Does this hasty reaction serve you? Is the swift automatic reply effective? We rarely pause to consider if our communication is effective. We assume we are good communicators, but this is often not the case. We often talk without paying attention to the consequences of our words beforehand. Sometimes we haven't fully listened. After all, none of us has attended listening school. Our reply and reaction may be based on assumptions of an implied criticism rather than the facts. Perhaps, you are like me and sometimes communicate in this manner too.

The solution is to try to remain calm, breathe deeply, keep your emotions at bay and check you've listened actively, ask questions if you need clarification, pause, consider different perspectives, chose your words wisely and then respond to the criticism. But, let's face it, this is tricky for most of us, myself included. So focus on baby steps, perhaps just work on taking a few deliberate breaths to slow you down, or focus on asking a couple of questions for clarification. Usually our emotions run in and take over our communication. Our reaction is immediate. Unfortunately, we haven't been taught how to work with and overcome the rush of emotions. I'm slow to improve in this area, but I rely on my meditation to give me a head start with calmness.

Listening

Listening is a valuable skill and asset in communication and just because we have ears does not mean that we have learnt to listen well. Our thoughts are forever active, flitting around wherever they wish to go. It is quite common that when someone is talking to us, our mind is thinking about other things, such as what to prepare for dinner that evening. And frequently our attention is not focused on the words the other person speaks; rather, our own thoughts have turned to preparing our own reply. Have you ever replied to someone without acknowledging what has been said beforehand by the other person? How often is there a battleground upon which all parties desire to talk and to be heard? Why is it that there is rarely a battle for the listening space? Perhaps we are developing as a society of talkers.

Inactive listening causes misunderstanding and can lead to conflict. We hurt ourselves when we don't fully listen. We may jump to conclusions and assumptions and swiftly react to implied criticisms even when they are not there.

Is it of benefit to you to slow down and listen fully? Here's a quick practice to help with listening skills. And it's very simple. When someone speaks repeat what they say, but repeat it using your own words. This means that you have to apply effort to listen to what the other person is saying. Surprisingly, you may find that what you repeat back isn't what has been said and you may need two or three attempts to establish effective communication and listening skills. This practise is especially helpful whenever you are perceiving criticism and judgement from the other person.

Conflict

Conflict usually occurs with people with whom we are close. Conflict is not necessarily bad. It can help us to voice some anger, negotiate new boundaries, communicate unpleasant feelings, resolve issues and establish new goals to move forward. Conflict can lead to cooperation and conflict can lead to harmony.

So why do so many of us dislike conflict? Perhaps it's in the habitual manner in which we conduct the conflict. Rather than re-enact our old habits in conflict situations, aim for fairness in its place. Allow all parties to express themselves. Establish a set of rules for conflict so that all parties feel safe, which include no violence, abuse, intimidation or overt aggression, passivity, and no shame. Also include any other guidelines which are important for you. Establish a signal, such as touching your right foot or saying a signal word, such as 'fish,' to indicate that you need time out for twenty minutes. Time out helps you to calm down. It is imperative all parties feel safe physically, mentally and emotionally and if you do not feel safe, be proactive and exit.

In conflict, there will be criticism. You will probably voice criticism and receive criticism. A helpful exercise to employ in times of conflict is the 'three, three' exercise. This exercise helps all parties communicate in a focused and effective manner. In this exercise, Person A speaks and airs his views for three minutes. After which, Person B mirrors back and repeats what Person A has said. Then Person B has a right of reply for three minutes, after which Person A repeats what has been said. This helps to slow the communication down and attends to the main areas of contention. It is respectful and all parties feel heard.

Sometimes, in conflict situation, you may continually feel unheard. You may feel that the other person is dismissing your point. If this is the case, repeat your point as frequently as you need to; rather than respond to questions or jibes, repeat your point until you feel heard. Stay with your point until it is delivered and understood.

Be patient and participate at a pace suitable and safe for you. Conflict does not need to be a criticism fest.

At your own pace

We walk, run, jump, dance and drive at different tempos. We perform quickly with some tasks while with some activities we work at a moderate or slow pace. For example you may have a quick mind, but act slowly with physical practises. When I am recording my lists of gratitude I write slowly and some days I don't act proactively at all, buffeted by the demons of ghosts past. The fact is, it doesn't matter what your pace and it doesn't matter if you become derailed along your path. We are all familiar with the saying 'life is a journey,' it's the same with beating the pain with the aim to feel better. There is no quick fix, feeling better is a journey. Perhaps we won't arrive at total betterment because we may find more layers to work with. Does it matter? Do you need a full stop at the end of your healing journey? Comas are fine, break the journey into short scenic walks and smell the roses as you go. This is the road to overcoming the pain and feeling better. Enjoy the ride, the result is worth it.

Feel the energy

Some of you will be adept at sensing the energy in situations around you. For example, you may be able to sense if an argument has just taken place when you walk into a room. Or, sometimes you may receive intuitions or energy impressions that a nasty person is maliciously trying to hurt you. If you are an intuitive personality type or if you understand and are able to work with energy, use this to your advantage. Stay safe, physically, mentally, emotionally, and spiritually and distance yourself from the energy of nasty people. At the same time, focus on your own energy. What energy are you presenting to the world? Be responsible for the part you play in these criticism dramas.

Therapy

For some people. The solution from the pain and criticism is therapy. A psychoanalyst perhaps or a psychiatrist. I've visited both and not always willingly. I visited a psychiatrist for a short while when my children were young. This was a stage in my life when I was working nonstop. I had a couple of art galleries in Sydney, and believe it or not, I'd opened another gallery on the other side of Australia, a four-hour flight away, as Australia is a big country. I employed a lot of staff, but my habit was to work hard. So I made and created a lot of work for myself. I wanted to be seen as a good girl and I thought I needed to work hard to be this. I wasn't thinking about happiness lists and I hadn't made my own happy goals. I was on auto pilot, working for the old outworn goals of money and success. Interestingly, all of my actions and daily scheduling always placed my children at the top of my list and gave my children most of my time. You can see the problem; my personal happiness and goals didn't align. I would sleep for five hours a night, but criticism from everywhere and my own inner critic was rampant. I ended up visiting my local general practitioner doctor, balling my eyes out. He was surprised, as he'd never seem me having difficulty coping with life's ups and downs and so he suggested I see a psychiatrist, as the first six visits are free in Australia! How did my time go with my psychiatrist? I can't remember. I can't remember at all. Blank

To add fuel to the fire, I decided to add voluntary charity work to my schedule. The only problem being that there wasn't a lot of free time on my schedule. So to fit everything in, I used to take my kids along to voluntary work on Saturdays. Once again my happy goals and actions didn't line up. I feel a need to help others and to give back to society, and this makes me feel happy. But this wasn't on my happy list. My meltdown was in full swing, criticism was everywhere. I was falling short at work, and work was how I measured myself. It was another three or four years before my partner, as nicely as he could, recommend that I visit a psychoanalyst, because I wasn't coping. I received this as an A grade criticism.

I stayed with Emma, my psychoanalyst, for about three years. She recommended I take Wednesdays off, to give me some time alone. I also learnt a lot about needs, something I had not considered.

Mind Games

What are your habits of criticism? Spend some time and carefully reflect: which remarks upset you the most? Is it remarks about your stupidity, weight, lack of contribution to the household, inconsideration for others, you get the idea. Write them down. Why do these criticisms affect you adversely? Can you trace this criticism back in your history? What are your triggers? Where are you especially vulnerable to criticism?

Unhelpful, self-deprecating and damaging beliefs about ourselves hurt us and we feel pain. What are your beliefs about yourself....are they helpful? Is it time to change them? In which areas of life are negative beliefs holding you back?

We can replace bad habits with good habits. If you need help to change your beliefs and mindset, consider to visit a qualified, respected therapist. This will help you discover underlying causes and patterns of behaviour which affect you.

What is the root cause of your pain?

We all have different types of pain; we have different issues and crises. The secret is to try to spot the cause of your pain. Is it physical, emotional, spiritual or mental? If you have mental pain, therapy is a good option for you. My own pain was spiritual. I can see clearly now that the only healer who was really going to help me was a spiritual healer. Doctors and analysts had little influence over my condition as my pain was in a different sphere.

Spiritual teachers

If the cause of your pain is spiritual. Get yourself off to a good, highly regarded spiritual school. You'll love it. You'll feel better. I remember learning about the energy body, auras and chakras and realising, for me, that it was a missing link. I reacquainted myself with my intuition, which I'd left by the wayside since Art College. Unbelievably, my natural clairvoyance returned on day one of spiritual school. I focused daily, sometimes more, on meditation and generally stopped worrying about criticism, as I now had a new hobby along with a deep understanding that I was on the right path and I was also having way too much fun. You'll know instinctively when you arrive with the right teacher or healer for you. You'll feel better.

Be the best version of you

Why do we spend so much of our time and energy in the hope that others will think well of us? This is a no win game as sometimes other people will not think well of us and think the opposite. Perhaps it's time to stop focusing on what others think.

Perhaps it's time for a radical change. Perhaps it's time to start loving ourselves. Consider to spend some time each day intentionally loving yourself and intentionally loving everything about yourself. Say to yourself, "I am marvellous. I love myself. I love myself all the time." Create internal love so you don't need to get it from others and then it won't matter so much if others don't approve or appreciate you. It is none of your business what other people think about you. It's your business what you think about you. It is your business to be the best version of you.

{ 7 }

Putting it to work Micro View (Up close and Personal)

Throughout the day, our attention runs free, un-tethered and unfocused. Where does your attention wander throughout the day? Do you direct your attention or is your attention restless and at the mercy of whims and distractions? For example, sometimes our attentions swirls around beauty, sometimes it is focused upon work, while at other times it may be focused on a conversation happening in the next room. You get the idea. For many of us our attention has mastery over us, rather than us having mastery and control over our attention.

In the same way we can harness and purposefully work with our attention to magnify the desires we have for happiness and our happy goals. Conversely, when we are in pain our attention aims and fires, straight like an arrow, for that which and who hurts us.

Where do you put your attention? Are you smelling the roses or pricking yourself on the thorns?

It is possible to train our attention so that it focuses on that which helps us. With daily effort and practise, we can train our attention to focus on the happy things.

Here is a selection of daily practises which have helped me and will help you too. Pick just one practise which appeals to you and action it. Even if it's just for five minutes a day, commit to it. Summon your power, summon your will, stand up and fight. Do you want the pain to go away? Do you want to feel good? It's up to you; the ball is in your court. Do the work. Pick one activity and commit to practising it daily. Frequent practise of new healthful and helpful habits gently changes us and helps us to feel good.

Daily Exercises

What do you want? What will make you happy?

These are simple questions, but it may be possible that you haven't asked these questions, let alone patiently reflected to discover the answers. We sometimes take the concept of happiness for granted without full understanding what it means. It can take a lot of time to write and record our true Happy List with happy goals. It takes careful reflection to really arrive at what will make us happy. Why not spend the time and write your own Happy List. See **Appendix A** at the back of this book for a Happy List Template to help you get started.

Read your Happy List daily

Writing up your Happy List is only part one of the process. The real work and this exercise centres on your commitment to read your happy goals out aloud once or twice a day. Simple as this sounds, it can be tricky to commit to this. It is easy to skip the simple exercises. But remember, sometimes simple is best. Simple works. Written goals help us. They give us clarity and direction. Goals inform us of an end destination to our journey. However, when we have written goals, we have a page of theory and theory doesn't create results—action does. The action which is imperative in this process is to read your Happy List aloud each day. Reading your Happy List aloud each day will help to keep your happy goals at the forefront of your mind. Then your mind can pay attention whenever opportunities arise to help you further your progress towards your happy goals.

In the past, I have found myself feeling anxious and uneasy about criticisms I have received. However, when I read my happy list, I can easily see that these criticisms are often centred on the small picture of my life. Amazingly, the subject and object of the criticism isn't bringing me closer to my happy goals. In fact, most of the criticism I receive, or even give to myself, has nothing to do with the happy goals on my happy list. This acts as a quick reminder to myself to leave the criticisms alone, and to stop my worry, as my distress is not helping me, but rather serving as a distraction from my Happy List. I stop in my tracks and remind myself to focus on my happy goals. These happy goals dismantle my pain, help me to feel good and keep me aware of the big picture of my life. Reading your happy goals daily will help you slowly turn your mind from the negative criticism you receive to feeling good.

Words of Inspiration to uplift your soul

Beautiful, inspirational quotes uplift out spirits. They act as an open doorway framing the beauty surrounding us. I usually post an inspirational quote once a day on my twitter feed. I do this for myself as well as my followers, as this practise helps me to feel good. The secret is to be intentional when you read the inspirational quote. This is an opportunity to slow down, 'smell the roses,' and place your attention on inspiring and uplifting ideas, revelations and creative thoughts. Take your time. If you hurry or read the inspirational quote mindlessly the opportunity is lost. Read the quote and lets the words flow through you. Notice where the quote resonates within your body and energy body.

Compile a file or scrapbook of your favourite quotes. You may find that you are attracted and drawn to particular themes, such as relaxation, creative expression, soulmates or music. These themes may indicate experiences in happiness which you are secretly looking for and perhaps haven't considered yet.

Many people like to use card decks to receive their inspiration because oracle card decks display beautiful imagery and provide tactile pleasure too. See **Appendix B** at the back of this book for a selection of forty wonderful uplifting inspiring quotes. And if you would like to see my card deck for daily inspirations inspired by my popular music posts, check out my blog. Surround yourself with beauty and positive inspirational words and notice how good you feel.

Affirmations

Daily affirmations work in a similar fashion to inspirational quotes. The difference is affirmations focus on you. Affirmations place their attention on the virtues you possess. Affirmations reaffirm your intrinsic, natural, healthy and beautiful character traits. Affirmations remind us of our inherent goodness, something we may need to be reminded of, especially if we receive lots of criticism.

The secret, again, is to read the affirmation with attention, focusing on what the words mean for you. With affirmations some virtues and qualities will resonate deeply. So consider honouring your intuition and emotional responses when working with affirmations. Perhaps some virtues will hold more significance for you than others. You may desire to cultivate some virtues and you may wish to magnify others in your life's expression. You may wish to vary the length you work with each affirmation. Sometimes your attention will be with one different affirmation a day, while at other times you may feel drawn to keep your attention gently focused with the message on a special affirmation for a week or longer.

With the practise of daily affirmations, do what feels right for you, as there is no set rule with methods of practise. There are also many wonderful affirmation card decks on the market for you to choose from. If you would like to see the I AM CARDS *Daily Affirmation card deck*, which I have designed especially for the purpose of feeling good check out my blog.

Daily visualisations

Some of you will have a strong visual sense, and may like to practise daily with this talent. Remember, the aim is to intentionally place your mind in a happy parking space. If your mind is spending more hours thinking about the good things in life and the things which make you happy, then naturally your mind will have less time to concentrate on the pain and the criticism you receive.

There are a few ways to proceed with daily visualisations. Firstly, remember back to your most happy memories. What are the happiest moments of your life? How old were you? Who were you with? What were you doing? What landscape were you in? What was the weather like? What were you wearing? What music was playing? With attention, remember all of the details. How did you feel? What was your mood? What were your emotions? Relive this happy memory as if you are playing the same role in real life, right now, in present time. Recapture the happiness you feel.

Another helpful way to work with visualisations is to draw pictures or to clip pictures from popular magazines of the experiences and material possessions you desire or need to make you feel happy. Add these pictures to your Happy List. For some people descriptive words conjure up the feeling of happiness and for others images are an easier way to feel emotions of happiness. Choose which method works better for you.

Gratitude—be kind, appreciate others. Allow the new wheel of karma to spin

This is a simple exercise that allows your mind to engage with and focus upon the wonderful episodes, possessions and events you experience in life and the positive qualities you admire and appreciate in others.

Take your pick, and start writing a gratitude list each day. You may like to use loose sheets of paper or a special gratitude journal for this purpose. Start each day with the heading, "I am so happy and grateful that,' and then proceed to write short sentences of the things you are grateful for. To begin aim for five or ten expressions of gratitude. As you settle into your daily practise your rhythm will naturally increase the number of gratitude's on your list. As you write, let your pen do the talking and try to keep the ink flowing on the paper, without lifting your pen. Authors call this 'Stream of consciousness writing.'

Gratitude and appreciation spin the wheel of karma. A marvellous mystical force is put into motion, listen carefully, be patient, and watch. As you sincerely and lovingly write your gratitude list and commit to a daily practise, you will notice the gratitude and appreciation returning to you. Was that a criticism you just heard from that nasty person, or, unbelievably, did he just praise you?

I am so happy and grateful that...

Self-love and ways to do this

Our days are busy. They may be filled with work, deadlines, tasks, commitments, duties and responsibilities. And if you are a parent or caring for an elderly family member, you may feel that your days are filled looking after everyone else, with woefully little time for yourself. I know how you feel as I've been in this situation too. If you reflect carefully you may find that you are continually playing the adult or parent role in your life. Perhaps you are in bad need of love. Perhaps you are crying out for some fun. If this is the case, now may be the time to focus some attention and love onto yourself, especially if you feel that you are not receiving this from elsewhere.

Consider how you can give love and attention to yourself. Do you enjoy warm baths with essential oils? Do you love the taste of fresh raspberries? Do you enjoy playing rock music on your guitar? Do you enjoy playing tennis? Pick an activity you enjoy and is feasible for you to practise and spend fifteen to thirty minutes each day enjoying yourself and giving yourself love and attention. You can mix the activities up too if you like. Remember, you are responsible for your life. You are responsible for how you feel. You have needs too. It's not a good idea to feel guilty taking some time for yourself and it's also not a good idea waiting for other people to pamper you as this may never happen. If funds are short, choose an activity which is free, such as a relaxing walk in a beautiful park nearby. When I was working and parenting my young children, the activity I craved most was solitude. I enjoy hobbies and active pursuits, but I crave internal peace more. When I am alone and in a relaxed state I feel love for myself and I feel rejuvenated. When I finally started to give myself this time I felt better.

Meditation

Meditation is becoming a popular practise. I love meditation. The root cause of my own personal pain was spiritual, so it's not surprising that my own preferred daily solution is spiritual. I started meditating about eight years ago. I was desperate for the pain to subside. I was willing to go to any lengths to feel better. I would have stood on my head all day if it helped conquer my demons. When I started my meditation practice I had to summon effort and I scheduled my meditation times, 8am and 3pm. I committed to the long haul. I knew there was no quick fix. I chose not to beat myself up if I didn't meditate on any particular day. I committed to five days a week being my minimum practise. Today, I have expanded awareness when I meditate. I am in awe when I meditate. I am in wonder. If meditation is for you, perhaps try a few different styles of meditation and pick the one you prefer and feel most comfortable with. Also, if you like, you can find a couple of guided meditations I have recorded for you on my blog.

Fresh air exercise

Some people prefer physical exercises to assist change. The aim is to create a new habit to refresh your approach to criticism, rather than substituting this with an exercise regime you currently practise. Spending time in the outdoors and being outside in the fresh air helps to loosen up our stagnant energy. Depending on your mood and natural inclination consider, walking in nature for 30 minutes, jogging in the outdoors, or a yoga class, if you prefer to work with a teacher. Concentrate on your breath and try to allow your mind to relax. Concentrate on the scenery around you and pay attention and appreciate nature. If music helps you to free your mind, by all means listen to your favourite playlist, with the one prerequisite that these songs do not conjure memories of pain. Choose uplifting music and because you are trying to create a new habit, this may be the perfect time to experiment and listen to new musical styles. Breathe deeply, rejuvenate and pay attention to feeling good.

Relaxation

Throughout the day we can become tense, both in our physical body and in our thoughts. Our mind can become filled with negative unhelpful chatter. Daily relaxation exercises help. They remove tension from our bodies and free our minds.

A wonderful and quick relaxation exercise is to sit quietly with your body relaxed and your feet touching the floor. Roll your shoulders backward and forwards three times to release pent up energy. Relax your facial muscles and let your jaw gently drop open. Place your hands on your thighs with palms upwards at the juncture of the thighs and the abdominal region. Close your eyes. Breathe in deeply through your nose and exhale through your mouth. As you breathe in visualise your breath gently sweeping away all the old, outworn, cobwebs from your internal body. Practise this slowly and consciously. For each breath, aim to inhale and exhale for about nine to twelve seconds each way. It is important that the breath feels comfortable and shorten the duration of the breath if the pace suits you better. With attention follow your breath around your internal body. After about three breaths you will notice that you start to relax. Practise this for as long as you like. I like to practise this rotation of the breath for about twelve cycles. This exercise doesn't take long, about five minutes; however, if you need a quick fix, one minute of relaxing the breath is fine too.

A nice addition, if you like to experiment, is at the completion of the breathing exercise and with your eyes still closed, concentrate and pay attention to one of your five senses. Choose hearing, touch, sight, smell or taste. Carefully pay attention for ten to sixty seconds noticing either; sounds, near and far, images and symbols your internal eye perceives, tastes and textures or smells and fragrances, or, the sensation and feeling in the centre of your palms. This is both a wonderful relaxing and calming exercise and will help to develop your intuition and awareness as well.

Music

A simple remedy to help calm your mind is to listen to some relaxing and gentle music. Music is one of the great healers in life and can quickly help to change your mood. If you are in pain, if you are feeling criticised, gather your power, be proactive and change the music channel. Remember there is nothing to be gained by ruminating over the bad times. When I am writing, I have a special instrumental soundtrack playing on my music system as this soundtrack helps to bring my thoughts, feelings and body to a state of neutral. I feel clear, composed and ready to receive inspiration.

Another proactive direction with music is to intentionally switch the music channel and listen to your favourite 'go to' happy songs. If you love music, give this solution a whirl. Once again, remember our aim is to take responsibility with feeling good. If certain songs help you to feel good, listen to them. Sometimes you may feel embarrassed with your song choices, but if they put you in a good mood it doesn't matter. It's your life. It's your mood. If you are feeling good, then there is little room for pain or criticism to enter. A secret between you and me is that I'm rather partial to 'Night Fever' by the Bee Gees......

Generally anything 80s disco hits the mark for me….shhhhh… don't tell anyone…

Humour—don't take it all so seriously

Humour is a wonderful and helpful tool. Have you had a laugh today? Did you see a funny post on YouTube? Have you read a humorous comic strip? Do you know any jovial people? Sometimes, with the huge doses of pain and criticism we receive we can become insular. We disappear inside ourselves. It takes effort to venture out and meet people. Depression can take over. It takes effort to seek out and read funny books, to see funny movies. It takes effort to see and feel the sunshine again. But the effort is worth it. Humour takes our mind of the pain and we feel better. We find that life isn't so bad after all.

In summary

These daily exercises are an example of easy practices you can follow to beat criticism and feel good. You may substitute any of these strategies with your own personal daily practises if you prefer. Choose to be proactive with your own happiness and select just one of these easy remedies as the first step. When you have mastered this solution and committed to a daily practise, include a second exercise to help you additionally free yourself from the negative clutches of criticism and to feel good.

The Last Word

To quote a line from the famous Greek philosopher, Aristotle, "Happiness depends upon ourselves." You deserve to be happy and to be happy depends upon you. Be bold and don't worry about what other people think. It's time to reclaim your power and beat criticism. We all deserve to feel good. It's our natural state of being.

I wish you love, joy, peace and happiness on your journey.

Appendix A

Happy List Template A

Happy GOAL Quadrants	
Health	*Relationships*
Career and finance	*Personal fulfillment*

Appendix A

Happy List Template B

Corresponding Life STYLE Quadrants	
Physical happiness	*Mental happiness*
Emotional happiness	*Spiritual happiness*

Appendix B

Words of Inspiration to uplift your soul

Daily Inspiration Quotes to help you feel good

"You can become happy just by deciding to be happy."
—Osho

"Happiness is when what you think, what you say, and what you do are in harmony."
—Mahatma Gandhi

"Be yourself, everyone else is already taken."
—Oscar Wilde

"Look deep into nature, and then you will understand everything better."
—Albert Einstein

"The more man meditates upon good thoughts, the better will be his world and the world at large."
—Confucius

"Remain calm, serene, always in command of yourself. You will then find out how easy it is to get along."
—*Paramahansa Yogananda*

"Happiness depends upon ourselves."
—*Aristotle*

"You must be the change you wish to see in the world."
—*Mahatma Gandhi*

"If a man does not keep pace with his companions, perhaps it is because he hears a different drummer. Let him step to the music he hears, however measured or far away."
—*Henry David Thoreau*

"He who hears the music of the Soul plays his part well in life"
—*Swami Sivananda*

"Just don't give up trying to do what you really want to do. Where there's love and inspiration, I don't think you can go wrong."
—*Ella Fitzgerald*

"Happiness is not a destination or an experience. It's a decision."
—*Carlos Santana*

"It does not matter how slowly you go as long as you do not stop."
—*Confucius*

'To avoid criticism say nothing, do nothing, be nothing."
—*Aristotle*

"There is a crack in everything. That's how the light gets in."
—*Leonard Cohen*

"The weak can never forgive. Forgiveness is the attribute of the strong."
—*Mahatma Gandhi*

"Find out who you are and do it on purpose."
—*Dolly Parton*

"Imagination creates reality."
—*Richard Wagner*

Don't criticize what you can't understand."
—Bob Dylan

"By three methods we may learn wisdom: First, by reflection, which is noblest; second, by imitation, which is easiest; and third by experience, which is the bitterest."
—Confucius

"The season of failure is the best time for sowing the seeds of success."
—Paramahansa Yogananda

"It does not matter if you are a rose or a lotus or a marigold. What matters is that you are flowering."
—Osho

"Discover yourself, otherwise you have to depend on other people's opinions who don't know themselves."
—Osho

"It is not in the stars to hold our destiny but in ourselves."
—William Shakespeare

"Raise your words, not voice. It's rain that grows flowers, not thunder.'
—Rumi

"Everyone has been made for some particular work, and the desire for that work has been put in every heart."
—Rumi

"If I were not a physicist, I would probably be a musician. I often think in music. I live my daydreams in music. I see my life in terms of music."
—Albert Einstein

"Logic will get you from A to B. Imagination will take you everywhere."
—Albert Einstein

"Without deviation from the norm, progress is not possible."
—Frank Zappa

"There are more love songs than anything else. If songs could make you do something we'd all love one another."
—Frank Zappa

"Don't compromise yourself. You are all you've got. There is no yesterday, no tomorrow, it's all the same day."
—Janis Joplin

"The meaning of life is to find your gift. The purpose of life is to give it away."
—Pablo Picasso

"If you want the rainbow, you've got to put up with the rain."
—Dolly Parton

"Kindness in words creates confidence. Kindness in thinking creates profoundness. Kindness in giving creates love."
—Lao Tzu

"Dance, when you're broken open. Dance, if you've torn the bandage off. Dance in the middle of the fighting. Dance in your blood. Dance when you're perfectly free."
—Rumi

"My soul is from elsewhere, I'm sure of that, and I intend to end up there."
—Rumi

"I'm not a prophet or a stone aged man, just a mortal with potential of a superman. I'm living on."
—David Bowie

"Sing like no one is listening, love like you've never been hurt, dance like nobody is watching and live like it's heaven on earth."
—Mark Twain

"Neither a lofty degree of intelligence nor imagination nor both together go to the making of genius. Love, love, love, that is the soul of genius."
—Wolfgang Amadeus Mozart

"Life is a song, sing it. Life is a game, play it. Life is a challenge, meet it. Life is a dream, realize it. Life is sacrifice, offer it. Life is love, enjoy it."
—Sai Baba

Acknowledgments

Over the years, I have learned from and been influenced by many individuals. I would like to acknowledge the following people:

My deepest thanks to my first spiritual teachers, my parents Frances and Thomas, and for all you've given me.

My very special thanks to my partner, my son and my daughter for bringing love, light, laughter, and joy to my life. Thank you Dave for your continual support and encouragement. Thank you for always being there to cheer me on! And thank you Berwyn for helping me with the written word.

A big thank you to all of my spiritual teachers who have guided me. My special thanks to Paramahansa Yogananda and Sri Yukteswar. An enormous thank you for your teaching, guidance and for accompanying me on this journey.

Thank you to The Divine for working through me. And most of all, I would like to thank, you, the readers. Your support for my efforts means more to me than I can express.

ABOUT THE AUTHOR

AWEN FINN

Awen Finn, who has been described as having a mix of Tina Turner's energy, Stevie Nicks' brilliance, and Ella Fitzgerald's range, was born in the United Kingdom and began her career in fashion before moving to Australia. In Sydney, Awen went on to develop a successful business in the art world, co-founding art galleries and a successful art publishing company.

Awen began her journey in spirituality after attending a meditation class with a friend. She went on to train and qualify as an energy healer and spiritual teacher before she began to understand the incredible connection hidden within music and the spiritual energy of the world. She now interprets how to apply this life-changing knowledge in people's favorite songs while completely transforming their understanding of music and its energy.

Awen's philosophy is if you want to be healthy, wealthy, and happy, you need to have as much insight into yourself as you can. Awen writes on personal development, personal growth, personal transformation, intuition, music and Song Reads™ Awen's goal is to create insightful, relevant content that you can put to work in your life.

Read other Books by this Author:

Read My Song, Read My Heart, Read My Soul Soul Music.

Contact Awen

To get the latest updates and resources visit:

readmysongreadmysoul.com

Awen speaks frequently on the topic of beating criticism and feeling good. She can deliver a keynote, half-day, or full-day version of this content, depending on your needs. If you are interested in finding out more, please visit her contact page at:

Readmysongreadmysoul.com/contact

You can also connect with Awen here:
Blog: www.readmysongreadmysoul.com
Twitter: twitter.com/ReadmySong
Facebook: facebook.com/pages/Read-My-Song-Read-My-Soul/1439109376353372
Pinterest: pinterest.com/ReadmySong
Instagram: instagram.com/readmysong

ONLINE COURSE

You've finished the book but do you want to take your journey with Awen to another level?

If so, then check out her digital course. The **How to Beat Criticism and Feel Good 6-part virtual course** is based on Awen Finn's book. This course, which you can do on your own time, will help you create beautiful, radical change by adding up subtle shifts every day and every week. Through each simple shift, you'll transform your life in awe-inspiring ways you may never have thought possible. Throughout the 6-weeks, Awen shares her personal experience of the *How to Beat Criticism and Feel Good* method and how you too can apply the book in your own life to help you achieve miraculous results in every area of your life.

SIGN UP NOW

http://readmysongreadmysoul.com/store-2/

INTRODUCING
MY NEW ETSY SHOP

Inspirational cards and art prints to uplift your Soul

I AM CARDS

Daily Affirmation cards to help you feel good

Visit

www.etsy.com/shop/ReadMySongReadMySoul

Surround yourself with beauty and positive
inspirational words and notice how good you feel

Have you ever wondered what your favorite song says about you?

Deep inside your favorite song lay the secret messages that unlock your psyche and all your potential. Song Reads are an awesome and fascinating way to discover your personality type so YOU can lead a life of happiness and success

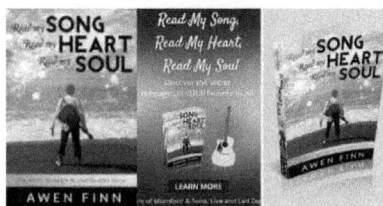

Sign up here to stay in the loop and to be the first to receive hot off the press notifications about new releases from Awen Finn and Read My Song, Read My Soul

Sign up here
http://readmysongreadmysoul.com

Now that you have finished reading the book

I'd love for you to leave a review on Amazon. It would mean the world to me.

Many thanks and Blessings

www.ingramcontent.com/pod-product-compliance
Lightning Source LLC
LaVergne TN
LVHW051130080426
835510LV00018B/2333